LITTLE MERCY

Winner of the 2024 Academy of American Poets First Book Award
Selected by Victoria Chang

Sponsored by the Academy of American Poets,
the First Book Award is given annually to the winner of
an open competition among American poets who have
not yet published a book of poems.

LITTLE MERCY

POEMS

ROBIN WALTER

Graywolf Press

Published by Graywolf Press
212 Third Avenue North, Suite 485
Minneapolis, Minnesota 55401

www.graywolfpress.org

Published in the United States of America
Printed in Canada

ISBN 978-1-64445-330-8 (paperback)
ISBN 978-1-64445-331-5 (ebook)

2 4 6 8 9 7 5 3 1
First Graywolf Printing, 2025

Library of Congress Cataloging-in-Publication Data

Names: Walter, Robin (Poet), author.
Title: Little mercy : poems / Robin Walter.
Description: Minneapolis, Minnesota : Graywolf Press, 2025.
Identifiers: LCCN 2024039923 (print) | LCCN 2024039924 (ebook) | ISBN
    9781644453308 (trade paperback) | ISBN 9781644453315 (epub)
Subjects: LCGFT: Poetry.
Classification: LCC PS3623.A446856 L58 2025 (print) | LCC PS3623.A446856
    (ebook) | DDC 811/.6—dc23/eng/20240911
LC record available at https://lccn.loc.gov/2024039923
LC ebook record available at https://lccn.loc.gov/2024039924

Cover design: Steve Halle

Cover art: Maksim Sokolov, *Abstract pattern on a tree stump*. Licensed
            under the Creative Commons Attribution-Share Alike 4.0
            International License.

—for Alastair Reid

—for my family

CONTENTS

Mercy bound, it binds.

—Dan Beachy-Quick

Lead me to the river with your mirror.

—C.D. Wright

LITTLE MERCY

—Here,

the body, yes,
sometimes

a river—little
mercy

—In the blue-

black mercy
between waking

& dreaming—
A wren

no larger
than a fist

flew to me—
lent my hand

her
gravity—

Rustle
of wings

in palm,
she made

my hand
a little nest.

Beyond the meadow

a thread
of moonlight,

there, tangled
in wet pine.

Rustle of wings
in dark

canopy—shadow
of wing

tip etched
into palm—

•

Each soul
that has nearly

slipped
the noun

of the body
remembers

river's
cold

mercy—

Every palm
touched by shadow

carries it—

The beginning of July

I thought I heard my mother crying,
but it was just the cold creek emptying—

●

At sunrise the chickadee pulls the morning open.
At noon, shadow of chokecherry slips across collarbone—

There are so many ways to want.

●

The wren weaves small feathers
& a little twine into her nest. The black heifer lows
for her calf drifting down valley. She looks at me—I pretend
innocence.

Flurry of small butterflies stills for a moment
on the purple phlox—
wings peaked into v's like the paper planes we sent stuttering
between desks when we were young—

We were practicing love, then grief,
then both.

●

Pronghorn. Honeybee. Ovum.

●

Each body decides its own way
through wind. The wood-rot corral finally gives
& leans heavy to the hoof-
stamped ground as if

in prayer. The aspen leaf rivers
the light, the horse arches her neck, whinnies,

picks her legs up tight & high—
the brook trout darts between cutbank
& stone—& the wren buries her body deep
into the bowl of her nest—pretends
her hollow bones heavy.

•

The pine needles gather pollen across the length of their spines—
a flicker shifts,
a yellow cloud blooms—

•

Bluestem. Meadowlark. Loam.

•

Spurge staked more hillside as its own this year.

Muddy lip of waterline lower than last.

•

Bloodroot & trillium.

•

Little songbirds make slender shadows—

I pretend my hand a nest.

•

In the slope of hill where we buried my uncle,
we leaned antlers careful
& neat against moss-
spottled stone.

•

Prairie smoke. Pasqueflower. Buttercup.

These the sounds we fold into prayer
& press into streams—

Penstemon. Lupine. Balsamroot.

Tiny heart. Sorry. Blood clot.

•

Heat lightning stitches across wide belly
 of sky—

—Little mercy.

•

Motherhood, a friend told me, will break the mind clean open.

This morning, held the empty hollow of a robin's egg in palm—
tried hard not to crush it. Crushed it anyway.

•

The seed head pulls the timothy sideways into an arc—

forms a little door to open.

•

This the season of miller moths & sorrows
edged into doorjambs & windowsills—

•

This morning, I prayed my body clean—

—clean & open.

•

Here, the stream refracts morning into light.

There, the hand gives way to body.

•

Meadow, you are enough to live next to. To live by.

—Watch

the faithful shadows
swivel around forest floor

—how gentle
the edges—

tilt the vowel skyward

like a little

hand mirror—

—hold bright
        the threshing sun—

Cinquefoil

If not
for these yellow

petals,

where would
small beads

of dew (little fists

of sun)
find a place

to rest?

All night I stayed
a body,

all night—

Would it be too much to say

the sun
pivots the morning

around the oxeye
daisies?

Watch it pull a slow shadow
across the field of timothy—

See it fleece
a thin rim of flame

through tree
line—The wet pine

needles must be shaking
the light.

●

Last night, I dreamt of digging
into a dried-up creek bed—

do not have the words to tell you
of the delight

when the water rose
to meet me—

What grammar for prayer?

Try:

The shiny black beak—
The heartbeat, a little soldier—

•

Try:

Switchgrass—miller moth—moon—

•

Try:

The moon is not a fist—

•

Try:

A fist of wet lilacs—

•

Try:

A fist of wet lilacs, shaking—

•

Try:

Nest—stitch—twig—

•

Try:

The whole thing backward:

Twig—stitch—nest—

•

Try:

Nest, on its own:

•

—Nest—

•

Try:

Nothing—not
naming
at all—

•

—

,

,

—

—Make

mouth
river

empty

   sky—

mercy, reaching—

There must be an animal come from there

Each time I see that big bush shake—
branches waving wildly—tiny leaves tumbling

the light—I think *there must be an animal
come from there*—wait

& wait—she never
arrives.

·

Astonishing the wide array of worms
the small wren carries in her beak

to the nest perched between the antlers
nailed to the porch ceiling—

Can't think of the word
that describes the sound of the chicks

newly alive & awake. Maybe like glass
clinking against itself—

or icicles breaking—but brighter,
truer—

She just brought a ghostly green worm
followed by a shriveled rust one—

Almost wrote russet but worried the word
too stately for a worm—but why not—she brought

a russet worm, then one shiny,
slick & black, obsidian—

•

Woke this morning thinking already of fall—
smell of grass curing copper

then blond—how the elks' bugle will first haunt the hills,
& then the mind—

Wonder which of the foals' ears
will split at the tip

come the first hard freeze—I get ahead of myself sometimes—

         sometimes, I am ahead of myself—

•

The wren stills for a moment on the flower box,
which I planted with lanky orange-yellow perennials

& short purple ones whose slim spiky petals
branch out like neurons

& which I bought because I thought them beautiful
& a little silly.

A fleshy pink worm, still flexing & curling,
dangles from the wren's beak—

She looks at me hard—measures me up
in an instant—my want

to make my body gentle; my love
for ripe peaches

& summer; how often, really, I want
to end my life.

•

Pretend her friendly & kind toward me—
but she is not. She is vigilant.

•

That big bush is shaking again. Its tiny leaves tumbling
the light.

Three birds

flying in & out
of the nest this morning—

One chick, quick little breaths,
hops & flaps between bush

& rock—from railing,
to table, to nest—

She tilts her head,
looks at me—

I ask myself gentle—
to cause no harm

here, but already
the small dog

comes trotting toward me
with a dark still mound

in her mouth—a chick,
I believe, from a different nest—

•

I catalog each harm
I've ever made with my hands

or mouth—the time
my father rose early

to make apple pancakes—
told him, please,

take me home
to Mom's—

the nights I'd sometimes hear him kicking
the goddamned-stupid-piece-of-shit dog

& sometimes how I'd slip
from my room, steel myself

to stop him, then couldn't
make the words—

empty-handed—

just looked—

•

Or the time I watched my neighbor
knock down the pigeon's nest

with a broom—one quick brushstroke—
crushed the little bodies

beneath a metal trash bin
so they wouldn't return—

Too messy, she said, *too
messy.*

•

The chick
now totters

on the sill
of the bucket

that holds the sun-
flower (small

wonder), she is trying out
its bouncy green arms—

•

I wonder if that old dog looked up at me
peeking over the banister—

small body—

•

Sometimes my father
would play

the piano
late into the night.

It was so

beautiful.

I imagined the notes
floating up the stairs

to me like little

bees—

—Even now,

farther
downstream

a duck's orange feet
churn the dark

waters

,   ,   .

—Lilies

bloom
across
shallow-

bellied pond
in the far-
off woods—

long lengths
of roots
drift.

Come
dark, white
petals

pull
close

—small fists

of night—

July prayer to survive the summer

Today was the first day I saw
the father of the chicks
come to the antlers—First,

he landed on the doorframe—looked at me
hard—before making the short flight
to nest—

The mother came busily on his tail feathers—
a small gray worm in her beak—
ushered him out of her way—

•

I wonder about the day
these birds will first
take flight—

which instincts they'll suspend
& which they'll trust—which of the tiny birds
will last the fall—

•

I am ahead of myself again—wanted
to tell you about instincts—how sometimes
they betray the body—no, sometimes

I betray the body—

•

The father is back again—nothing in his beak.
Their chirps are so much louder today—almost like tiny bells,
or water spilling—

•

Here, there is a father.
There are not always
fathers—

but always, birds,
& sometimes, yes,

a window.

•

My mind flips to a line
I love: *You can fall a long way in sunlight.*
You can fall a long way in the rain.

—Night rivers

mouth

 mercies

quiet
      tongue—

Last night

in my dream
I could not

think,
could not

recall
the name

of the little bird
that hops around

the currant bush—small
body twisting

the apricot
morning—

Trimming the tomatoes

Worried the cows
that pushed through the sawbuck fence
would eat the first tomato (small

miracle—a body born
from nothing). They preferred
the thin-lipped petunias

I potted while thinking of my uncle
whom we buried
in the hill.

When I was small,
I'd send him long
letters

addressed
to Tank, his big black horse
I loved—

Tank, I'd ask,
are you happy
to be a horse?

Are you—

I must have suspected,
even then, the need
to bury the scissors so they are not—

so they are not so close to me—

when trimming back
the tomatoes (small

miracle).

All along

The dogs root around
in the cool dark
beneath the porch—

Thought I heard the thrum
of a hummingbird come to try out
the red flowers, whose name

escapes me & whose petals
are already curling
in on themselves—

All along it was the thin drone of a plane
drawing geometries across the pale face
of morning—

July heat mixed up
with the building whine
of crickets—

·

Grass grown so high now the little dog
has to leap into a wild pirouette
just to see across the field, pink ears waving madly—

(the wish

to see—)

·

Peonies. The name
of the red flowers, I remember,
is peonies.

Proximal worlds coupling briefly

In the heat of afternoon sun,
twin pronghorn antelopes

flit the line of their gaze
between me & their mother—

Catching my scent, the mother
pauses, stills, looks at me

hard—The commas
of her ears pin me

to the still hot day of a shared world
with no common tongue—

She spins
& disappears over lip of hill,

twins rippling
behind her.

•

Back home, cricketsong
slips between timothy grass—

Beyond the wet meadow, the sound
of nothing.

How far from here

Killed the jasmine again.
At first, it seemed not to mind so much
Wyoming & its always wind

shuffling through pines.
But its want for warmth
betrayed it. Oh little jasmine,

we can pretend
against it,
but the body wants.

The birds in the nest are quiet now.
I saw them this morning—five wiry frames
huddled against each other for warmth.

The mother busy
& vigilant—one black eye
peering at me over the lip of nest—

When wind riffles
timothy, insects still
for a moment

before starting up all over again.
First hint of fall in the aspens on my walk home,
one yellow flare—bold & quick—

•

Little wren—
Wide wet meadow—

How far from here
to over there?

Robin has always been my name

It's true
I feel a kinship
with birds—

as if my mother knew
I'd suspect the body begins
at wingtip—

Maybe it has less to do
with the name
than how earnestly

I wish my mouth
around the little
trill,

the quavering *s*
held briefly & waterly
               in the teeth—

                    •

Sometimes,
I cannot recall
my own name—

I mean, sometimes
can't sleep, can't
speak,

forget
all about
wrens—

Still, the day opens. Call me
meadow. Call me horse.
River, call me—

Last July light

Cattails slice

into yellow belly
of moon.

The cricket stills.

•

Scissor-tailed flycatcher

threads the horizon,
stitches it

to sky—

The ouzel needles in & out

of river—delights
in the arrival

downstream—

•

The bronze-bellied

hummingbird slips in & out
of the peony, the jasmine

sends a green shoot

up the crumbling
wall—

•

The poorwill ripples

the still night open—The tree
line caesuras the dark stamp

of sky. The wet pines shake—

•

My grandfather

sits on his hands to hide
their trembling. Somewhere, a bull

bellows. Last of the lilies bloom—

•

Wind threads beetle-

thinned timber & the dark
storm opens

its belly.

•

The sow bear shuffles

through brush. The horse catches
her scent, flares her nostrils,

makes her body

still.

In the dry season,

timothy grass
comes into the sleeve

of its stem

& the creek slips

underground
without anyone's

noticing.

—The body

rivers open—

each of us
undone

by shadows small
& shaking—

—One morning, a fox

in the middle
of the road,

wind lifting golden
his hair, a little

blood rivered the edge
of his mouth (small

teeth)—scooped
his body soft

& careful—placed
him gentle

alongside
the sage-

brush, left a purple
flower near

his head (sharp,
tufted ears).

•

—Quiet wind, pale-bellied
moon, blood rivers

the mouth—

—Make

this mouth
a red oak

leaf—
—listen,

stay the sight
to the clean

horizon, see
the moon

unfold
the hand

as it pulls
the body

into the next
season—

How the letter *h*
reaches upward,

downward,
both—holds

the body
open, holds

it gentle
as a leaf, shaking—

—Last night, I dreamt

I was moving
the gray mare

to new pasture (better
grass), she spooked

& reared—her body split
in two across the steel fence—

my hands could not couple her
together—

•

Years ago, early summer, tied
a rope to the bay's slender

leg, let out a few lengths,
staked rope

to ground—did not know
his leg would break

at the cannon
bone—

•

Later that night, a comet
traced the ridgeline

as the bullet rivered
his skull—

moonlight swiveled
in two small ponds—his eyes—

Windowsill of night, clear glass pane of grief—

Had it in my head to write a poem that begins:
The windowsill of night, the clear glass pane of grief—

Wanted to start the poem
where these two things touch—

or really where any two things touch:
the soft feathers on the wren's underbelly—

how maybe they're layered on top
of one another like spoons in a drawer—

Or the gymnastics of the letter *j*
—how it hooks down, sinks

knowingly below—but more beautifully,
how the dot above does a wild leap—

a spark boring a tiny hole
into night—

•

Begin again—while picking raspberries
yesterday I wanted to hold in my head

the delicious names of the things I saw
so as to fold them into a poem later. Here:

Snowberry. Baneberry. Dwarf daffodil.
Wild clematis. Tanager!

•

Start over. Imagine it like this:

An exclamation point walks into a bar
& sits beside the letter *i*

i says: *you're doing it all backward—*

! replies: *doing what backward?*

Life, i says, *You're doing this whole life backward—*

•

Didn't realize until just now what this poem wanted
to excavate:

The tugging fear that I am—

•

Try again. Woke this morning
& stepped outside to check on the wren's nest

—empty.

•

Still quiet air.

—Sometimes, cold river

mercies
  tongue

& moon

rinses
wrist—

—Early September

scatters beneath
the box elder

like a spilled
alphabet

—Vein

of yellow
aspens

splits
the mountain

dark—

—Consider

the riverbank—
how it loosens a little

beneath the slender-
legged doe—

See her wet nose
reflect the morning—

—Search for a coherence

of self, some
form

shaped by
the things I love—

dust-drenched
light through

rafters,
smell of leaf-

litter,
the pines—

—Close the eyes

& still can hear
the *tok tok*

tok of woodpecker
piercing bark

for beetles—needles criss-
crossed along spine

—Long-bodied

pines cross-

hatch
the understory

until they return
to sky

as smoke

—Elk-

rivered wet
mountain,

antlered
hills,

little rivulets

of rain, cold

It is fall again

& yes, I am lonely & yes,
the beetle kill pines

sparked like matches—

Red disc

of sun on smoke-
silled horizon.

·

The day opens almost as if
the whole forest

hadn't burned—as if ash
were not falling

like snow—

Cheatgrass. Deadfall. Longing.

The whole hillside licked clean—

We pray the littlest things

Smear of yellow
petals

across wet
mountain

—first snow—

—Dreamt the body

river beneath
bluish snow—

the mouth a nest
of shadows

thrown by slim needles
of pine, shaking—

—Consider

the bulrush—how it bends
toward the given

ground below November
snow—

Hold gentle the name

Did you know the robin
will cover the faces

of the unburied dead
with leaves—or

sometimes,
moss—

•

Almost, a loneliness—

•

Here, on earth,
we honor our dead

by holding their names
gentle in our hollow mouths—

•

This morning, found a picture
 of a dear friend's sister,

gap-toothed grin, tucked
between the pages of a book—

the refrain *by her own hand*
nettles the mind

bare—

Thin river held quiet
beneath tongue

—In the barely wind

a thread
of milkweed

uncouples

from dry cradle
of husk

Pray not to behold

but to be held by—

Meadow cupped by bowl of blue sky
wind rivering quiet

then quick
through lodgepole pines—

—Look there, at the familiar

shadow etched
beneath

timothy—

watch it spin
the day around

its stem—

hold the minor entities
in your mouth, yes,

but do not say them—

·

,   -   ,   .

& if love

is a little barn

swallow—raising

her nest high

in the rafters,

—hold—

—The vole edges

through snow
across

wide altar
of night —

Barred
owl loosens

from
branch—

Iris
widens

in needled
dark—

—It is snowing, again

each flake
a seam

of sky split

open—

•

The bough breaks,
makes a little

steeple—

—Sometimes, river

shreds
moon

into bright
ribbons

that lift
the body

     beneath

—Across snow,

winter shadows
deepen—

—longing
to be a nest,

the hand folds
open

at night

—Slender-fingered

shadows slip
across upturned

wrist—

—At the edge

of the pine,
a little snow

lifts

—Something here about memory

If you root around
hard enough,

of course you will find
the letter that begins

the body—at least
what you now know

of it. Something here about
memory—or something

about the wound itself
bearing the body—

by which I mean giving birth to it—
as if a dark leaf

unfurling, or a hand
opening to itself—

—Pray the body stay

awake if only just to see
snow lift

from moon-
bright branch—

—wide mercy

of morning, come

Small reverie

of nest—

If I could make
myself so true

a shelter, palms
pressed

—Sometimes, if you keep still

enough, you will find
in your dark mouth

          a moon—

        •

Shadowless, the light
today—

          Merciless, the songbirds
come too soon—

        •

A wren is no larger than a fist.

        •

Yellow winter,
          make of me a room—

& if

the rafter
belongs (if only

briefly)
to nest

& the hand
to the beautiful wrist—

& if the comma
anchors,

& the noun
lifts—

if language
keeps us

& couples
us, see

the little
wren

lift

from thin river
of moon-

light held
in palm—

Mercy of meadow

covered
in snow,

fleck
of mica

edged
in granite

offers
the quarter

moon
back to itself—

•

In the morning,
light rivers

the body
edged

in water—

wide nest
of palm

cradles
the river-

rinsed
face—

•

The sun

(a little
mirror)

opens

eye—

NOTES

In grateful recognition of influences & inspiration:

The opening lines of "In the blue" are indebted to Yusef Komunyakaa's "The Blue Hour" in *Night Animals* (Sarabande Books, 2020).

"Cinquefoil" is for Susannah Lodge-Rigal.

The lines "You can fall a long way in sunlight. / You can fall a long way in the rain" are from "August Notebook: A Death" by Robert Hass; the title "July prayer to survive the summer" is indebted to his poem "Songs to Survive the Summer" in *The Apple Trees at Olema: New and Selected Poems* (Ecco, 2010).

"Last July light" is for Danny Schonning.

"In the barely wind" is for Emily Spiegel.

"Pray not to behold" is for Skeeter Johnston.

"Sometimes, if you keep still" is for Kristin Macintyre.

"& if" is for Jack Fields.

ACKNOWLEDGMENTS

Grateful acknowledgment to the editors of the journals in which many of these poems first appeared: *Poets.org, Reliquiae, Seneca Review* & *Wildness*.

My deepest gratitude & immense thanks are owed to Victoria Chang, for finding in these poems something to share & for the luminous words that grace this cover. You have lent me the gift & honor of a lifetime. Thank you.

Thank you to Jeff Shotts for your generosity, your time, your care—thank you for turning such a carefully attuned ear to this work. Thank you to Carmen Giménez, Nirali Sheth, Brittany Torres Rivera, Marisa Atkinson, Caelan Nardone, Veronica Silva, Claire Laine, Casey O'Neil, Yuka Igarashi, Katie Dublinski & the entire Graywolf team for welcoming me into the pack, for ushering into the world such vital & vibrant works, for all you do for language & those who build a life in it.

Enduring thanks to Ricky Maldonado & the Academy of American Poets for the incredible gift of giving these poems a home, for opening such a wide & generous door for this work & for all you do to sustain poetry in the world. Thank you for the reminder to hold close to heart the Gerald Stern lines, "Lucky life is like that. Lucky life. Oh lucky life. / Oh lucky lucky life. Lucky life." What a wild bewilderment & happiness. Thank you.

For the bright gift of your words, thank you Kazim Ali & Carl Phillips.

Thank you to all my past & present teachers, for everything. Thanks especially to Jeff Hooper & Katherine Halsey. Endless gratitude to Jim Moore, Dave Mason, Jane Hilberry, Sarah Vap, Prageeta Sharma, Sasha Steensen, Camille Dungy, Matthew Cooperman & Harrison Candelaria Fletcher for modeling how it is we might build a life in words & lift one another up along the way. Thank you, too, to my students.

For all my friends at work in language, you inspire me—Becca Spiegel, Jess Turner, Alick McCallum, Hannah Bright, Esther Hayes, Katherine Indermaur, Maren Schiffer, Carly Fraysier & Arnisha Royston. For your company & care along the way, thank you Chelsea Davenport, Alex Tarika, Molly Sinnott, Claire Hester, Olivia Wall, Jack Fields, Natalie Selzer, Meredith Dworkin, Douglas Land, Denali Gillaspie, Kate Dunn, Michael Hunter, the Meadow Witches, Michele Bush, Lisa Romasco, Laura & Martin MacCarty, Aubriee McGinty, Bergen Swanson, Kristy Beachy-Quick, Tara Furey, Nadine Lehner, Madi Manson, Meriwether Hardie, Julie Liebenguth, & Sophia Cinnamon. Thanks to my uncle Greg for the gift of binding books together.

Special thanks to Eleanor Anderson, Carmen Taylor & Megan Hooker. Thank you for your good & true hearts; you are so dear to me.

For the little mercy of your friendship & for helping me build this book twig by twig, thank you Danny Schonning, Kristin Macintyre & Susannah Lodge-Rigal.

Bright gratitude to Dan Beachy-Quick, without whom I wouldn't have known how to open to the song that comes when we learn to listen— for teaching me to trust the small nouns crying faith.

Thank you to all the animals who've made me & especially to Fiddle & Banjo for being such reliable & funny friends. A whistled trill of thanks to the little wrens under whose nest I wrote this book & under whose apprenticeship I learn to sing.

Thank you to every single poet who's ever written a word & to the many, many writers whose language & thinking have shaped my own. As Ross Gay writes, "My breath is made possible by the breath of others . . . we owe each other everything." How true.

My thanks & my love to Alastair Reid, to whom this book is dedicated.

& most importantly, boundless thanks to my family—Mom, Dad, Bob, Kaitlin, Anna, Logan, Reilly, Liza, Jenk, Darin, Miles, Lucas; every single Walter, Tudor, Johnston, Twombly & McNair too numerous to name—you are my anchors in & to this world. It is such an honor to love & be loved by you.

Special thanks to my uncle Skeeter for keeping me company at the Saddle, my granddad for sharing his love of mountains, my sisters for their love, my dad for his music & my mom for showing me how to be an artist.

& full-throated thanks to you, reader, for spending your time with these words—

ROBIN WALTER is a poet, book artist, and printmaker. Her writing has appeared in the *American Poetry Review, Poets.org, West Branch,* and elsewhere. She teaches at Colorado State University and lives in Fort Collins, Colorado.

Graywolf Press publishes risk-taking, visionary writers who transform culture through literature. As a nonprofit organization, Graywolf relies on the generous support of its donors to bring books like this one into the world.

This publication is made possible, in part, by the voters of Minnesota through a Minnesota State Arts Board Operating Support grant, thanks to a legislative appropriation from the arts and cultural heritage fund. Significant support has also been provided by other generous contributions from foundations, corporations, and individuals. To these supporters we offer our heartfelt thanks.

To learn more about Graywolf's books and authors
or make a tax-deductible donation, please visit
www.graywolfpress.org.

The text of *Little Mercy* is set in Minion Pro.
Book design by Rachel Holscher.
Composition by Bookmobile Design & Digital
Publisher Services, Minneapolis, Minnesota.
Manufactured by Friesens on acid-free,
100 percent postconsumer wastepaper.